What's Become of Eden:

F Poems of 1 Family

at Century's End

STEPHANIE STRICKLAND

Stephanie Strickland's book of poems, *True North*, won the Poetry Society of America's Di Castagnola Prize and appeared as the Sandeen Prize volume from the University of Notre Dame Press. Electronic *True North*, published on disk by Eastgate Systems, won the *Salt Hill* hypertext prize. Her other books include the Brittingham Prize-winning *The Red Virgin: A Poem of Simone Weil*, University of Wisconsin Press, and *Give the Body Back*, University of Missouri Press. Her work has received many awards including a National Endowment for the Arts poetry grant, a National Endowment for the Humanities fellowship in hypertext poetry, a New York Foundation for the Arts poetry grant, the Open Voice Award of the West Side Y Center for the Arts in New York City, and a poetry grant from the New York State Creative Artists Public Service program.

What's Become of Eden:

F Poems of 1 Family

at Century's End

Edited by
Stephanie Strickland

The Hudson Valley Writers' Center, Publishers

WHAT'S BECOME OF EDEN: POEMS OF FAMILY AT CENTURY'S END

Copyright ©1994 by Slapering Hol Press
Design: James Laird

Special thanks to the poets who contributed their poems and to the following people who participated in the production of this publication: Margo Stever, Barbara Nackman, Geri Rosenzweig, Anneliese Wagner, Dare Thompson.

First edition published in 1994. This second edition in 1999 is made possible with generous assistance from the Thendara Foundation, the Westchester Arts Council, the New York State Council on the Arts, and individual contributors.

ACKNOWLEDGMENTS: **The Moment** by Len Roberts. First appeared in *Poetry*. Copyright © 1988 by Len Roberts. Reprinted by permission of the author. **Grating Parmesan** by Barbara Crooker. First appeared in *The Denver Quarterly*. Copyright © 1991 by Barbara Crooker. Reprinted by permission of the author. **The Window** by C.J. Hannah. First appeared in *Hob Nob*. Copyright © 1994 by C.J. Hannah. Reprinted by permission of the author. **A Father's Vacation** by Cris Mazza. First appeared in *The Contemporary Review*. Copyright © 1990 by Cris Mazza. Reprinted by permission of the author. **When the Call Came** by Norbert Krapf. First appeared in *Blue Unicorn*. Copyright © 1983 by Norbert Krapf. Reprinted by permission of the author. **Thinking Tristan James or Meredith Rae** by Deidre Pope. First appeared in *Sojourner*. Copyright © 1991 by Deidre Pope. Reprinted by permission of the author. **Mother** by John Gilgun. First appeared in *Amythyst*. Copyright © 1990 by John Gilgun. Reprinted by permission of the author. **What the Dollmaker's Children Hear** by Hilda Downer. First appeared in longer form in *The Charlotte Poetry Review*. Copyright © 1993 by Hilda Downer. Reprinted by permission of the author. **Grandmother** by Nancy Roxbury Knutson. From *Nothing Should Fall to Waste* (Arts Wayland Foundation, 1983). Copyright © 1983 by Nancy Roxbury Knutson. Reprinted by permission of the author. **Grandchild** by Maxine Kumin. From *The Long Approach* (Viking Penguin, 1985). Copyright © 1985 by Maxine Kumin. Reprinted by permission of Viking Penguin, A Division of Penguin Books, USA, Inc. **White Apple** by Dennis Saleh. From *Palmway* (Ithaca House, 1975). Copyright © 1975 by Dennis Saleh. Reprinted by permission of the author. **Father and Children** by Peter Cooley. From *The Astonished Hours* (Carnegie Mellon U. Press, 1992). Copyright © 1992 by Peter Cooley. Reprinted by permission of Carnegie Mellon University Press. **Tree House** by George Keithley. First appeared in *Ararat*. Copyright © 1985 by George Keithley. Reprinted by permission of the author. **Nesting Dolls** by Neva Hacker. First appeared in *The Child* (Mayfield Publishing Co., 1985). Copyright © 1985 by Neva Hacker. Reprinted by permission of the author. **Conjugation** by Martha Collins. From *A History of Small Life on a Windy Planet* (U. of Georgia Press, 1993). Copyright © 1993 by Martha Collins. Reprinted by permission of University of Georgia Press. **What Difference Does It Make?** by Natasha Sajé. From *Red Under the Skin* (U. Pittsburgh Press, 1994). Copyright 1994 by Natasha Sajé. Reprinted by permission of University of Pittsburgh Press. **Exile's Child** by D. Nurkse. From *Isolation in Action* (State Street Press, 1988). Copyright © 1988 by D. Nurkse. Reprinted by permission of the author. **Four Hours** by Denise Duhamel. From *Smile!* (Warm Spring Press, 1993). Copyright © 1993 by Denise Duhamel. Reprinted by permission of the author. **Walking in Holcomb Gardens** by Alice Friman. First appeared in *Texas Review*. Copyright © 1986 by Alice Friman. Reprinted by permission of the author.

ISBN 0-9624178-4-X

Slapering Hol Press, a project of The Hudson Valley Writers' Center, Inc.
300 Riverside Drive
Sleepy Hollow, NY 10591

Cover photograph by Lynn Butler, "Sleepy Hollow Morning." Courtesy of Lynn Butler.

Peter Stockton Reed

December 7, 1953 - May 1, 1994

CONTENTS

ONE

The Moment   *Len Roberts*   11

Grating Parmesan   *Barbara Crooker*   12

Home   *Floyd Skloot*   14

Wrestling   *Mark Solomon*   15

The Window   *C.J. Hannah*   16

A Father's Vacation   *Cris Mazza*   18

You had the choice, Martha   *Vivian Shipley*   20

When the Call Came   *Norbert Krapf*   22

Thinking Tristan James or Meredith Rae   *Deidre Pope*   24

Terra Incognita   *Lee Patton*   25

The Relenting Son   *Frank Van Zant*   27

TWO

Islands   *Geraldine Connolly*   31

After the Last Great Anti-War Demonstration   32
    Sean Thomas Dougherty

Epithalamium   *Zev Levinson*   34

The Flight Home   *Penny Cagan*   35

Mother   *John Gilgun*   37

The Day After   *Anne McCrary Sullivan*   38

Bass Lake, California, 1973   *Kjersti A. Reed*   39

What the Dollmaker's Children Hear   *Hilda Downer*   41

The Safest World   *Alice B. Fogel*   43

The World Forgetting by the World Forgot   *Gary J. Whitehead*   45

Maternal Legacy   *Judi K. Beach*   46

Grandmother   *Nancy Roxbury Knutson*   47

Grandchild   *Maxine Kumin*   48

White Apple   *Dennis Saleh*   50

Father and Children   *Peter Cooley*   51

School Bus   *Kirk Nesset*   52

The Alcoholic's Lament   *Susan Richardson*   53

The Day We Knew Michael's First Tooth Was Loose   54
    Maria Theresa Maggi

Tree House   *George Keithley*   56

THREE

Nesting Dolls   *Neva Hacker*   61

Jane's Gifts   *Nora Ruth Roberts*   62

Conjugation   *Martha Collins*   63

What Difference Does It Make?   *Natasha Sajé*   64

Babysitting at the Plainsman Motel   *Alissa Reardon*   66

Exile's Child   *D. Nurkse*   67

Four Hours   *Denise Duhamel*   68

Where God Lives   *Jeanne Bryner*   69

Family Gathering   *Amorak Huey*   71

Walking in Holcomb Gardens   *Alice Friman*   73

ONE

THE MOMENT

Walking the three tiers in first light, out
here so my two-year-old son won't wake the house,
I watch him pull and strip ragweed, chicory, yarrow,
so many other weeds and small flowers
I don't know the names for, saying *Big,* and *Mine,*
and *Joshua*—words, words, words. Then
it is the moment, that split-second
when he takes my hand, gives it a tug,
and I feel his entire body-weight, his whole
heart-weight, pulling me toward
the gleaming flowers and weeds he loves.
That moment which is eternal and is gone in a second,
when he yanks me out of myself like some sleeper
from his dead-dream sleep into the blues and whites
and yellows I must bend down to see clearly, into the faultless
flesh of his soft hands, into his new brown eyes,
the miracle of him, and of the earth itself,
where he lives among the glitterings, and takes me.

—Len Roberts

GRATING PARMESAN

A winter evening,
sky, the color of cobalt,
the night coming down like the lid on a pot.
On the stove, the ghosts of summer simmer:
tomatoes, garlic, basil, oregano.
Steam from the kettle rises,
wreathes the windows.
You come running when I reach for the grater,
"Help me?" you ask, reversing the pronouns,
part of your mind's disordered scramble.
Together, we hold the rind of the cheese,
scrape our knuckles on the metal teeth.
A fresh pungency enters the room.
You put your fingers in the fallen crumbs:
 "Snow," you proudly exclaim, and look at me.
Three years old, nearly mute,
but the master of metaphor.
Most of the time, we speak without words.

Outside, the icy stones in the sky
glitter in their random order.
It's a night so cold, the very air freezes flesh,
a knife in the lungs, wind rushing
over the coil of the planet
straight from Siberia,
a high howl from the wolves of the steppes.
As we grate and grate, the drift rises higher.
When the family gathers together,
puts pasta in their bowls,
ladles on the simmered sauce,
you will bless each one

with a wave of your spoon:
"Snowflakes falling
all around."
You're the weatherman
of the kitchen table.
And, light as feathers,
the parmesan sprinkles down,
its newly fallen snow
gracing each plate.

—Barbara Crooker

HOME

More than fear,
more than the feeling
of flying through air
and reeling
off the hard edge of the sink,

what this photograph of me
at three
years old
with a fresh black eye
and forced smile
brings back is the deep
sense that I could not do
anything right,

could not keep
them away or think
straight enough
could not move
fast enough
to stay clear
of the hate
always roaring around
something still
at the cold
center of our life
they called love.

All I knew
is that I could not be
myself and be safe
while
they were anyplace
I thought of
as home.

—Floyd Skloot

WRESTLING

In their mother's queen-sized bed I
wrestle my two sons—Jonah Nachum, dove
of comfort, dove of rest and return,
Benjamin Joseph, son of my right arm,
son of the true wife, added on to me.
This Sunday afternoon, first winter chill
sharp, sliding off the windows, we tickle,
squeeze, grapple with each other, till
we can hardly breathe for giggling.
Then my sudden stillness makes them wonder—
I smell my father's pipe smoke drift
from the living room of forty years ago,
hear the crumpling of newspaper stuffed
under kindling, a blue tipped match
scratched against the fire-place brick
as bright November sunlight bends down through
dark spruces in the next-door neighbor's yard.
Warm air rises over little yellow flames.
Thin strands of fragrance twine through slanted
orange light. Steam from cups of heated milk.
Ghost! Who is it, you or I, preparing
incense in the outer chambers of the past?
In arms and legs of these boys now
remorse as ash, as vapor vanishes. Here alone
within this nest of generation shall we
clasp each other and take rest.

—Mark Solomon

The Window

Roy, Mother spoke softly,
her back to us as she washed
the supper's dishes. Dad
sat at the round oak table, reading.
Roy, I would so like a window here,
above the sink. It's so dark and no
amount of lighting seems to help.

Ummm, He mused, looking up
as if studying the problem.
Bad time of year for that.
The first frost'll be here this week.

I looked at the wall wondering what
mother wanted to see out her window...
the peach orchard, now autumn barren,
and a mile away above the orchards,
the bookcliffs looming
like monstrous battleships.
In spring she'd see pink blossoms,
fragrant clouds caught in the branches,
in summer, dark green leaves curling
finger-like 'round the swelling fruit,
and in fall, along the canal,
cottonwoods exploding into a yellow
so bright it hurts the eyes.

Spring eased into summer,
the peaches ripened
from almond size
to that of baseballs.
Dad came in for lunch one day
and stopped, stunned,

just inside the door. A faint cloud of
white dust drifted in the air, and a
smell of wood long hidden from the sun.
A ten pound sledge hammer lay on the floor.
Mother stood near the sink, staring sharp eyed
at him, as he stared at
the hole smashed in the wall
above the sink, dripping white chunks
of plaster and laths.
A gentle, warm breeze blew down the canyon
and through the hole
filling the kitchen with
the smell of ripening peaches.
Mother pointed to the ragged hole.
That is where I want the window.

—C.J. Hannah

A FATHER'S VACATION

To pack the trailer took him all night
the night before we left
on our camping vacation, two weeks
every summer, five kids in a station wagon,
tents, coats, sleeping bags, propane stove,
black skillet, canned food.
After the rain trenches were dug
around the pitched tents, he began
to carry big rocks into the cold,
quick river, laying them across, side by
side, slowing the water just
enough to make trout pools.
He fished early mornings then again
at dusk, working
both sides of the river.
Without a shirt, while chopping wood, a
muted shout from his chest, the
ring of the ax, but few
words. His beard grew.

He packed his saw into
the woods to cut logs he
lugged or dragged back to camp,
brought jugs up the side of a mountain
where a spring surfaced, drinkable
water, three gallons on his
back, one in each arm. He hooked
trout then thrust the pole into
our hands to land the fish, exhaled
sharply, a nearly inaudible
grunt, when we flung the fish out of the water
backwards over our heads, tangling
fish, line and pole in
the heavy brush. A few times

each camping trip, he
made pancakes on a sheet of shiny metal over
a fire pit built with rocks so everything was
exactly level. He poured big
perfectly round pancakes, nothing
fancy, none shaped like
Mickey Mouse. Standing in the firelight
in a blue sweat suit, the bowl of batter
in one hand, spatula in the
other, the blood of a fish
still on his arm from the morning's
catch, he made pancakes
without smiling.

On a big rock between two trees, we
wore out the knees of our jeans, got
sap in our hair, on our arms. It smelled
thick and piny, turned black
and tacky (and later he
would have to use gasoline to
scrub it off). He
walked back and
forth, past the rock, gathering
dry greasewood for kindling, a red
bandana around his forehead. We played
with kids from other campsites and
glanced up at him as he
passed, but never shouted, "Hey
Dad!" nor waved, and
one little girl said, "I'm afraid
of that Indian." Later
I pushed her off the rock and
my father sent me
to my tent.

—Cris Mazza

You had the choice, Martha,

as you clocked second month,
gut: firm flat dinner plate
or inflated rubber glove.
Despite their warnings, you
did not have him sucked out,
preserved in saline to let
the doctors sample fetal bone.
You lugged yourself proudly,
an elastic of Siamese skin
upholstering your bodies
until his hunger cored you.

Blasphemy of love you
cannot now abort: Lesch-Nyan.
One in one hundred million
but when it is yours, a statistic
is not a number but your son.

Your heart burns at his whisper,
words that bother him so
on that irreplaceable face.
You do not love him less
for the caged heart or because
he must always be lifted
to the van, have his hands tied
so he will not scratch out
his eyes, his teeth pulled
to stop him from gnawing his arm.
Scars are the letters you must keep
him from learning, knowing he
is taught nothing by the pain
but that it feeds his need
which can never be filled.

Spoon him your dreams, even
though your son tricks you

and spits them back on the tile.
Slip, slide, skate through
those dreams. Lift your arms
as if you were an angel in flight
in spite of what you do that
is so human: buying the blue bicycle,
propping it in his room, building
a ramp although you know he will
never pump or brake, flinging gravel.

—Vivian Shipley

When the call came
I was about to cut the grass
for the first time. Wild
onion and dandelion were
sprouting across the lawn.
Sheaths of lily of the valley
bearing round green bells
were surrounding the lilac.

When the call came
the yellow marsh marigolds
were rising like the sun
against a boulder in
the flower bed. Bees
buzzed around bunches
of purple grape hyacinth.
The operator said, *I have
a collect call from Colombia.
Do you accept the charges?*
I replied, *Yes, I accept.*

When the call came
the leathery leaves
of bloodroot along the ledge
of the stone wall were
wrapped around stalks
like green sheets on which
white petals lay. Beside
the fishpond the fronds
of maidenhair fern were
unfurling in the sun.
A voice with a Spanish
accent spoke in my ear,
*This is a social worker. We
have a baby girl born eight
days ago. Will you accept her?*

When the call came
the white blossoms
of the wild cherry at the edge
of the woods were fluttering
on black boughs. The tips
of Japanese irises were
pushing through the soil.
Specks of Bibb lettuce
lay like green confetti
on the upper level of
the rock garden. *Yes, we
accept her*, I said. *Yes*.

—Norbert Krapf

You'd think it would be so easy.
Just a trip up the mountain and a focused
mind. But we don't find babies so simple.

My mother is sewing bears
on the bibs she makes for proper
babies—not ones who come from borrowed
sperm. I say, "We're thinking of having one."
She looks confused, then smiles, "Yes, a party
this summer. That would be nice."

But that is not what I've said.
We will not have a party
until after the birth, when T.J.
or Rae is safe in our bed.
When we are fresh in love
with the way our baby smells,
with this new job of motherhood.

For now we debate the options—
an egg in a dish, baster full
of cum, releasing you
some nights to one friend
or another. If it were up to me,
there would be no intrusion of science
or brother's blood. Just the two of us
in blue print skirts, walking
all day to reach the summit.
And we would focus on your belly
as I braided your hair, invoke
the pregnant Muse with her wild success.
I would slip my hands under your skirt,
make our bodies a circle
until we could feel the first quick
flutter that would swell you full
of that new, perfect beauty.

—Deidre Pope

This should be the way home
but where the Mother Lode flattens,
the landscape's alien, altered.
Those foothills were never anybody's
mother—how could these drought grasses
have sustained us? This almost Ethiopian
October heat breathes wildfire
all across California. Beyond
plowed-under farms, the lion-colored Buttes
claim to be the seat of gods. Piles of ash,
mute erosion, what strike can they make
against evil? What stake in good?

Shadows linger in the dying
shade of oaks or lurk barely seen,
just ahead, across the highway.
Predators? No, don't lie with metaphors—
it's a virus. God, please,
what the hell's become of Eden? Is that Eve
setting the table in that farmhouse window?
Or is she the one, miles and miles farther,
leaning toward her dying son? She's had so much
to grieve: his sight, half his hearing, all
his mobility, the company of his laughter,
and finally, tonight, the presence of his mind.
And yet, for the love of God, her grieving
hasn't even begun. Where the highway
finally unravels into darkness,
my high beams scan redwood ridgetops crazily
as lost brothers' flashlights, switchback
after switchback dropping me closer to the shore, home
to harbor where in the morning my mother's on my arm
at Mass and the sermon falls like ashes:
"You're not good enough."

After lunch, my father takes me to his church—the river—
where the blackberries still cluster over his dock.
I haven't been home in blackberry time for years,

feasting as I clamber down to take my brother's place,
helping my father move the boat to its winter mooring.
We jump—the summer dock's towed out from under us.
I fumble with the knots. My dad doesn't mind:
"You're doing good enough."

Blackberries spill on my brother's tray.
Can't get his mouth around the damn spoon,
so I help him shovel in the last mouthful,
then yank off his sticky t-shirt and help carry him
to his daybed. "Those berries...I picked 'em for you,"
I mutter, wondering how much he can hear.
"They were good," he groans. "They were good."

—Lee Patton

THE RELENTING SON

My hand extends skyward above my baby's eyes,
my fingers wave separately, arrhythmically,
like distracting kite fringe popping silently above.
His eyes fix on the billowing hand, this signal for sleep time that we share,
and, this time, this wild wired-up gassed-up little zoom, relents,
relaxes, accepts.

To reinforce what he sees, I whisper:
peeta peeta peeta peeta peeta peeta peeta—
I don't remember how this strange language began but
he likes this sound, this noise which comes from the sky; I am
a yard full of birds who sing in his subconscious like a drug.

In my arm's crook I collect him now, rainwater fallen, softly pooled.
I pause before lifting him to the crib, running one delicate finger
along the thread of his wet jaw. His mouth wants to open, stops,
obeying his heavy eyes, his greater need. It's time; he is ready to sleep,
and I am thinking about what babies must dream when I am startled
                                        I am startled
                                        by ANGER I am
                                    ANGRY right now!
                                in bad dreams,
                            my dreams,
                        his hand comes down
            a different way. Father's hand is a hunter, a bird of prey swooping
        to grip to catch to claw to rip me apart and feed to his nest;
        father flew away when I was five father flew away when I was five.
    Where are you now?
now that my son is here?

One day, I will hold you, my startled father, I will
hold your grey head in the crook of my arms,
raise my hand above your sleepy eyes,
wave my fingers, separately, arrhythmically, I will
whisper strange sounds, I will
forgive you forever in this language of tongues.

—Frank Van Zant

Two

ISLANDS

Somewhere there is this frightening
home movie. I am thirteen.
It is summer, my hair long, tangled.
My mother butts against me, playfully
at first, then harder. She is pulling me
into the mother and daughter photo,
a film meant to record us, happy
in summer, in the Thousand Islands
but catches instead my furious face,
arms tightened around my own shoulders,
then her pulling my arm too hard,
pulling me down the rocky hill
of our vacation into the camera lens
where green pines swing fragrantly.

I have almost escaped but my mother
grabs my long hair in her fist,
pulling me to my knees. A fighting fish
she's hooked, I'm ferocious, refusing
to be her prize, ready to strike her.
My arm's raised. Why hasn't my father stopped this
film? He could have stepped from behind
the armor of the camera and put his hand
between us. Can't he see a wall
must be put up, a barrier
across our furious wishes. Two islands
that have grown together, we can't
separate. We each face head on
that part of ourselves we hate,
mirrored in the other.

—Geraldine Connolly

AFTER THE LAST GREAT ANTI-WAR DEMONSTRATION

The brass buckles
On blue coveralls,

Bright as medals,
Shining on the shoulder straps

Of that young man
With his hair cropped,

Chewing spit
As he pumped our gas.

I was six, maybe seven
When my step-father opened the door

Of our rusty Chevy, his afro
Round as the moon, & that man

Glanced at my mother & said,
"That's a fine white woman

you got in the car, boy."
And the acrid smell—

Like a match being struck,
As my step-father stepped

Up an inch from his eyes,
And whispered, *"That's*

My wife..."
And then took out

His wallet, & paid him;
Then he started the car

And drove us north to
Ohio, far away

From that EXXON sign
Just outside D.C.

—Sean Thomas Dougherty

EPITHALAMIUM

For Andy

Andy Fuckin' Frank, you're doing it!
Of course your love is the ultimatum.
But marriage, on February 2nd? You know a lot of weirdness
happened on that day: my half-birthday, Raymond's death,
pagan seasonal *sabbats* festival,
Mr. Groundhog looking for his shadow,
the igniting of the cushion in our dorm room
from the sun refracted through the hanging
stained glass butterfly.

That labyrinthine letter
explaining the politics of your ceremony:
Suzy doesn't want her brother's wife up there, the bitch,
so I agreed to have Suzy's brother on my side
then Scotty and Guy
and she can have her friend from Sweden and
her sisters. That's it (hope I didn't lose you).
I hope you understand—
I wanted you to be in the wedding but
I think this may be the best way to solve the puzzle.

Andrew, you know how I feel about formalities
and flash; I didn't even go to our graduation. What matters,
and I know this from 20 years of brothership, is you playing
your electric guitar—bent over in concentration,
black curls in your eyes, fingers spidering,
tuned to the strings, gone from our world—
so that nobody, not even your wife, could possibly interrupt your song.

— Zev Levinson

34

The Flight Home

When the fog walls in the Philadelphia airport
like a shutter folding against the wind,
when your flight is cancelled and your wife
goes into labor back in Los Angeles,
and you spend the night
in the lobby of your conference hotel,
are you the same boy who performed tricks
with your magic wand, black top hat, and cape?
Are you the same boy who turned yourself
on and off like a robot when I rubbed your nose,
and spit out your "knock knock" jokes?
Are you the same boy who sat with me
after school on the stairs of our dark house
with your legs swinging through the guard rail,
waiting for our passed-out mother to awake?

When your plane takes off with a blind puff,
and the crossing of the country is nothing
but six lost hours from coast to coast,
do you feel tight in your skin
and bury your head between your knees,
the way we did when we sat in the back
of the old red station wagon holding
our breath, counting the curves
as Mother veered from curb to curb
through the drunken suburban streets?
When you finally cushion yourself into a seat
with your legs spilling into the aisle,
does the silver buckle that cuts across your waist
feel like the cool rush of Mother's wrist
as she stood above you each night with a belt
and snapped?

When you descend through the black sky,
when you fly home to your wife,
who walks herself to the hospital

while her water springs by the cupful,
when you fly home to your daughter
who cannot wait the full nine months to see the world,
when you make it just in time
to count each contraction, each heartbeat,

are you the same little boy
who was locked out on the porch
when you talked back to Mother,
are you the same little boy
who was stripped of your clothes,
and made to stand naked through the hours?

—Penny Cagan

MOTHER

Your wrist was stiff and you threw a softball
like a man.
My wrist was as limp as embroidery
and I threw like a girl.
When I lisped in your presence,
you cracked me on the head with your knuckles
and said, "Sissy!"
You could make a muscle
but I could only attempt one.
I was your panty-waist skinny-bolink,
your hipless wonder, your *Jaqueline*.
You swung through the 1940's
in your Persian lamb, so confident,
like Joan Crawford in *Mildred Pierce*.
You wore a slave bracelet on your ankle
but insisted you were no man's slave.
Drunk on rum, you drove the Ford too fast
down the back roads of Reading, Massachusetts,
while I screamed to be let out.
"Only sissies scream like that."
You went out to work as a waitress
leaving your apron and a note for me:
"Thaw out the frozen peas, feed the kids,
do the dishes, tidy up. Love, Mother."
At twelve, I fell in love with my best friend.
You saw, you understood, you made your prediction:
"Life is going to be very hard for you."
But this little faggot fought for you.
When Dadda had you down, that time he broke your nose
so that the blood ran over that Persian lamb
ruining it so that you could never wear it again,
I threw myself at his back, I hung on there,
pulling at his face, screaming
until he threw me off, smashing me
against the kitchen wall.
I did that for you. *Me!* Your sissy son, Jack.

—John Gilgun

THE DAY AFTER

The day after
the telephone call
    "We don't want you to worry,
    your son is all right,"
struck me with absolute knowledge
that he wasn't,

over and over I hear his attackers,
    "Goddamn nigger lover,"
over and over their shifting forms
distort above his crumpled shape
and I see the heavy boot,
the heavy boot...

At this time of year
when he was small,
we would take night walks.
We smelled mimosa
and approaching rain,
listened for the owl
of the tall pine.
In moonlight

       the heavy boot
advances toward the softness
of his cheek, his eye, nothing
nothing can stop this motion
nothing can keep it from repeating
and repeating and repeating.

           —Anne McCrary Sullivan

BASS LAKE, CALIFORNIA, 1973

For Douglas

With the pines' breath
mixed with incense
cedar, it seems impossible
Doug can only gasp.
That old brown belt, still warm
from his father's
waist, has looped his neck
like a silk tie, its X
slid against his windpipe,
squeezing it into spasms.
I rush him out of the cabin
into open air, as if all that abundance
could save him. We sit
down by the volleyball
courts, where nights, families
from the campground
hoot and laugh, and bats
swoosh like Frisbees.
I hold his shoulders
until tears don't spurt
and his seven-year-
old voice can ask, "Why? I was only laughing."
This time I mouth
no excuse. Now, when I see us
walk back to that cabin,
I want to shout, "NO!
We can do it better without him,"
but I don't know that then.
We walk back slowly, into three
more years—the red rose
bushes along the brick
fence he'd rip out
to spite me, the nights
I'd rush all three

kids to the car, and he'd follow,
calling them,
and the rainbow
of calendulas I'd plant
fresh from flats. He'd yank
each one from its new
bed, flailing them wildly
against the house, all that dirt
showering, darkening
the grey of the front porch.

—Kjersti A. Reed

WHAT THE DOLLMAKER'S CHILDREN HEAR

You shiver in bed recalling the news report
of a father scalding his baby to death.
You pulled your children to you
until your heartbeats synchronized.
They may not always be this safe.
They will one day cross a street alone,
maybe in a city they have traveled to by air.
You consider all the scraped knees,
broken grapevine swings, dating,
as you hold the round shields of your pupils
up against the vast darkness.

One in a million is what your foster parents called you.
You made the grades, sang in choir, drew the best in art
so that you could excel in survival.
You were not the people you came from,
not like the other foster children.
You were one in a million,
and your children would be happy.
They would be the wonderful people the world needed
and they would not have to hear the screams
behind their own closed door.
You would be the moon breaking the night cycle.

Your parents sent your brother to his death
on a dark night,
on a bicycle with no brakes and no reflectors
up and down the long hill to the store
for a loaf of bread,
that clinging soft impression of life.
Zane was twelve, your idol, with twinkling white teeth
and with dreams of becoming an astronaut artist.
The driver didn't see him,
but you do, over and over,

the waxen doll in the open casket,
the slamming of the door.

A piece of muslin is nothing.
It is a limpness of the imagination.
On the table, it calls itself simplicity without shadow.
Held to a window, it only addresses the function of a curtain,
but when you cut out a small pattern of the body,
sew and stuff it tightly,
paint the eyes with matching blue vanity,
and design a bright wig of yellow yarn,
you make a piece of muslin breathe alive.
This is your magic, your talent,
the spark through your fingers,
creating happy children with pink embroidered smiles.
Once, you sewed a music box inside
just when you thought you had lost all power and light,
and you were amazed that with the turn of the key,
you could make a simple piece of cloth sing.

—Hilda Downer

Darkness is your silk scarf, a soft disguise inside which you hide,
little one who takes cover, who loves closets and curtains,
loves to hide without being sought, and lie still,
somewhere inside somewhere, in pleased silence:
inside you is the memory—I carry it for you—
of a darkness darker than pre-birth.

Now you reach so gladly to close yourself in, a re-birth,
and before the door closes I witness the smile you think you hide,
which is all for you, for the embrace of air that you
gather against your face. Or under the bed, its curtains
of fabric down, hems brushing floor, you crouch in silence,
not waiting, suspended in some deep, some still

unnameable pleasure, and there you will stay, as still
as moss in shadow, and for as long, until the birth
of satisfaction releases you from out of that silence
or some other kind of hunger sends you out of hiding
to find me on the other side, so strangely free of curtains
or shade, under the beam of burning lamps that you

like to leave. In your secret places, deep sea treasures, your
patience is as infinite as the dark, your heart still
pulls your blood through tunnels warm as bedsheets, and the curtain
of your breath waves invisibly, in and out, like birth.
Darkness is the anchor trailing daylight, following—but first hidden—
in day's wake. For you, a place of peace and silence.

I want to bridge my arm through that silence,
through your own dark passing of time, to offer you
an arc of twilight, a road opening across the high
pitch of night, a pier to the rise of a future day that I still
insist upon. But you hold on to the darkness, giving birth
to it with both hands. You stay behind your curtains,

and I don't know—should I reach in past the curtains,
should I "find" you, pull you back out of that silence,
and hold you close again, body to body, just like at your birth,
your small self full against my longer one, so that you
might remember the world of solid arms, the hold in which you still
fit, the one I have for you? Or should I let you hide,

trust your bright curtained eyes, full of the excited peace you hide
like a secret from birth?— As if the safest world for you
were this dark and silent one you will make as long as you still can.

—Alice B. Fogel

THE WORLD FORGETTING BY THE WORLD FORGOT

In her neat house on the last street
with any dignity my grandmother must
sit in her mahogany rocker and count
the ticks of the grandfather clock,
little chips of the unremitting chisel
that whittles away a shape's significance.

Not a place of thought, but of solicitude,
walls and shelves burdened with tokens
and old photographs, a brooding space
where the spoken word is heard as seldom
as the phone rings and as often as the rain
brings back the voices of restless children.

Is it her sacrifice, then, to remain
the dividend, to mete out to those
who have a share in her what effete
faculties she clings to till the last
swing of the heavy pendulum? And who
holds stock in an old and broken woman?

Is she as ashamed as I am that we've
never known one another? I'm not sure
of her age, and I don't know her address,
but I'm certain that her backyard ivy grows
wild, that my father by now has forgiven her,
that once, simply a child, I could have loved her.

—Gary J. Whitehead

MATERNAL LEGACY

My mother says she had no parents,
but I know better. I have seen
their faces, and I know their names.

Her sister handed me a photograph
with edges brittle as fall leaves
and said, "Here are my parents."

I gently bent the folded corner
back, hoping it may have covered
some message meant for me.

Thomas was seated on a wooden crate;
Annie Sara stood beside him, sleeves
rolled to her elbows, some dark skirt.

I couldn't clearly see their eyes
for a shadow, like a sepia caul,
wrapped them in this paper birth.

Of them I have nothing: no letter,
no scented pipe or seasoned skillet,
no heirloom, not one thing.

All I have is the great desire
to be hugged by them just once.
When I show this photo to my mother,

she says, "I had no parents,"
and turns away.

—Judi K. Beach

GRANDMOTHER

Your children bring you to a nursing home.
A clean one
where the people speak Spanish.
It's your home town
so old friends can visit.
If any are left.

Last time I saw you
your eyes had retreated
into your skull.
You kept seeing things we couldn't.
The cracks in your skin
had grown so deep. Quietly
you wrestled.

You will die soon, I hope.
After an evening of rain
when the desert smells clean,
iglesia bells resounding in the village.
Your mind will become clear.
Faces will match names, places:
the evil daughter and the good
will be one again,
your one, beautiful daughter.

You will smile.
Laugh maybe.
Even forgive us.

—Nancy Roxbury Knutson

GRANDCHILD

For Yann

All night the *douanier* in his sentry box
at the end of the lane where France begins plays fox
and hounds with little spurts of cars
that sniff to a stop at the barrier
and declare themselves. I stand at the window
watching the ancient boundaries that flow
between my daughter's life and mine dissolve
like taffy pulled until it melts in half
without announcing any point of strain
and I am a young unsure mother again
stiffly clutching the twelve-limbed raw
creature that broke from between my legs, that stew
of bone and membrane loosely sewn up in
a fierce scared flailing other being.

We blink, two strangers in a foreign kitchen.
Now that you've drained your mother dry and will
not sleep, I take you in my arms, brimful
six days old, little feared-for mouse.
Last week when you were still a fish
in the interior, I dreamed you thus:
The *douanier* brought you curled up in his cap
buttoned and suited like him, authority's prop
—a good Victorian child's myth—
and in his other hand a large round cheese
ready to the point of runniness.
At least there, says the dream, no mysteries.

Toward dawn I open my daughter's cupboard on
a choice of calming teas—*infusions*—
verbena, fennel, linden, camomile,
shift you on my shoulder and fill the kettle.
Age has conferred on me a certain grace.
You're a package I can rock and ease
from wakefulness to sleep. This skill comes back
like learning how to swim. Comes warm and quick
as first milk in the breasts. I comfort you.
Body to body my monkey-wit soaks through.

Later, I wind the outside shutters up.
You sleep mouse-mild, topped with camomile.
Daylight slips past the *douane*. I rinse my cup.
My daughter troubles sleep a little while
longer. The just-milked cows across the way
come down their hillside single file
and the dream, the lefthand gift of ripened brie
recurs, smelly, natural, and good
wanting only to be brought true
in your own time: your childhood.

—Maxine Kumin

WHITE APPLE

The cow with a hole in its side listens,
the new baby is crossing the road.
Where they've put the ground he steps
lightly: one tree, a long row of vineyard,
one belt whirring "grapes, grapes, grapes."

Every night he takes the steps inside.
When the night comes up it casts the moon
out in front of the baby, and he is like
a scrubbed piece of moon, light in the dark
as the future comes up out of the ground.

Men in lizard skins have gone on
the long way before him, leaving milk.
They went on into the rest of time
but they saw the hunger making milk.
Now anchors from the rest of time

hold the morning underneath the earth.
Stars are shining. Food is shining.
In the chill grey of faint dawn
the new baby stirs. He is the white apple
broken loose falling a long way.

—Dennis Saleh

FATHER AND CHILDREN

Sometimes taking my son's hand at night
to lead him outside where the moon awaits us,
he dawdling, then toddling beside me, babbling,
the ghost child waits at the opening of the door.
She is dead, she is what only his mother and I
know about; she sits on the bottom step
spitting, *Get on it, I've been waiting*, shredding bark
from the azalea bush or tossing stones in her fist
at the streetlight, *You're late, that son of yours*
held you up, and she stands then, exposing a face
where I could weep as the clouds pass over it,
the eyes and mouth sockets of darkness moonlight sucks.
For Christ's sake, you haven't got forever,
she shouts, the shout echoing down the street
where all three of us start out, night after night,
to wear out my little one until I pick him up, nodding.
And she is always ahead of us and behind,
she is on all sides, spectral and tireless.
When we arrive at our door, she gives us the finger
with a fleshless hand dissolving in the streetlight's glare.
Tomorrow, if we're lucky, will be her night off,
she has time. She's got all oblivion to be jealous of him.

—Peter Cooley

School Bus

Pain is the green and white school bus I kissed Gerri White in,
"breaking her in" as I actually said in my cruel-minded
eighth-grader way—a bus with no seats, red curtains, two sets
of plywood-and-foam-rubber bunks, pillows big as small planets,
and maybe a sprig plucked from a field, something leftover, blue lupine
drying to pieces, there in the jar by the sink. Pain is the alive-dead
net of the daydream, an ongoing affair with regret.
My parents, not hippies like Gerri's folks, but trying on life-
styles for weekends, sold the old bus, sold
the 1950 Dodge pickup I drove as a learner and later
drove through a barn, sold the rust-red house in the photos,
the shivering ferns and trees by the creek, the clamor in winter.
Now they are gypsies. Campground to campground they drift,
nosing into Wisconsin, Montana, deep into Oregon
amongst dented bread trucks and mastodon vans, pausing
beside the gray track of coast highway, hunkered in mist.
Lately, odd mornings, I stand in the doorway, away
from the mirror, away from my drawerful of photos, and almost
decide, odd moments, that loss is relief. I almost tell myself
this: Either squint and keep squinting or choose to stop looking.
Let the tilting continue, see it all tilt and upend, or bone-pale
with smiling, quietly enter the easing, this overdue easing,
this slow breaking in to break free.

—Kirk Nesset

THE ALCOHOLIC'S LAMENT

I remember my children best
as they were when they were young:
flitting like butterflies within the fence
in their new Easter clothes, losing their balance
on Sloans Lake ice, tossing bread to the ducks
who flocked there in the fall. Now only Trudie visits,
she with her religious, and not daughterly, intent.
Why the others close their lives to me I can't recall.
Perhaps they blame me for missing that one Christmas,
not many years past, when I fell asleep
in a friend's locked bathroom, having had too much to drink.
Fran says they found me hugging the toilet for comfort,
and I arrived home too late
to watch our kids open their presents.
(It's not the only time, I'm told,
my memory went bankrupt.)
What I recall today are Susan's birthday picnics—
on some windy mountainside we'd spread our blanket,
anchoring it with rocks, or at Morse Park
we'd ride the horse swings.
Beyond that my mind's a blank.
The faces of my two youngest daughters blur.
In their pictures they shoot baskets
or lob tennis balls, though what game they won
or which one I attended I couldn't tell you.

—Susan Richardson

THE DAY WE KNEW MICHAEL'S FIRST TOOTH WAS LOOSE

was a Sunday, and I do the laundry
and eight other things while he plays
outside Sunday, little boys banging up
and down the apartment stairwell with
balls and arrows and a cord of string to
fix the bow, and the target, too, when I insist.
There's a hard game of spy with the bigger
girls across the complex going on, and
he is breathless and red with involvement
each time he falls in the door to gather another
part for an imaginary or real apparatus.
Nevertheless, the law of even our
debauched Sabbath dictates he must
stop and have lunch. He's probably hungry,
adrenalin and intrigue aside, because he
throws himself down at the kitchen table,
breathing heavily in wordless consent.
He looks a bit like he's been
quarrying marble or sandstone.
His dirt coats him, like magic, initiate
to the secret rites of Playing Outside.
His eyes are glazed over in sacrificial piety.
He eats strictly for the glory of What Comes After.
Extraneous conversation would
cheapen this sacrifice, so I simply say
"Pick two things that aren't pudding or licorice."
As I'm slicing the perfunctory
cheddar cheese and cucumbers, he stops
chugging his juice to say, "My tooth hurts."

"When will it happen, Mom?" he has asked me daily
in the car, in the bathtub, on the way to the mailbox,
at the table, doubting me more each time I
say "It's inevitable," because Tyler and Carl
have already beaten him, lost two or three,
even though he is six-and-a-half, will be
seven this August, and we're pushing May.
"What does *that* mean?" he sulks, heartless

and untiring in his quest for hard facts,
ever watchful of how my big words can elude.
"That means it has to happen, nothing can stop it,
like the way you keep asking."

I appreciate his longing much more
than he suspects, and privately
wash in the sadness of knowing it's
the very beginning of a beard he will shave,
keys to the car, and women who will have answers
I can never be asked to give.
From the corner of my eye,
shrubs and gnarled eucalyptus trees
outside the apartment window wave at me
from the breeze and murmur a wordless chant
in their slower kingdom, perhaps to comfort
those of us without roots who move so fast
and so often through the structure
of our own cells that sometimes
just living we frighten each other.

But today I'm chopping and ignoring
all that sentiment, I'm just Mommy
with one more thing to do, saying
"Well, open your mouth, point to which one."
Oh but then our eyes hop a boxcar
together and we both hang on,
air and years streaming around us,
because in this instant truth from his body
breaks Michael free, and I see
in his smile when he jumps on his own,
the ground of his life leaping
under him wildly as snowmelt does
when it roars over granite, rife with
the danger of promises or beginnings,
his timing and his feet will know
when to feel sure.

—Maria Theresa Maggi

TREE HOUSE

1
All morning with my wife I labored
over that house, then left it
for our children
to devise the door. Left them, too,
the rope ladder. Still its spiral rungs
like stigmata burn
the pattern of their purpose in our flesh.

Together on the porch we take our rest—
We climbed so long
in and out of that tree
my arch bears the ache of each branch
underfoot. Unable effortlessly
to open, my palm remembers the grip
of those limbs, the hammer, the rope.

2
Like trout our children float in the shadows
of forked boughs. In the bare-bones house
built of baling wire, weathered wood, leafy roof,
nothing more substantial than their dread
of falling hard to the earth forms
their floor. They hide their faces. Headfirst
they emerge, they splatter paint on the door!

They cry—first fright, then joy!
Leaves glow with glee,
feet and hands learn the boles
that bear weight. Up and down
the trunk and leaping
branches, laughter crawls
across the cool afternoon.

3
Shadows flood the grass and sink
the odd artifacts
of our hours: hammer, handsaw, paint-
brush stained blood
red. Ruler, pliers. Paper
plates, plastic cups. The bucket
of chicken bones plucked clean at supper.

Forgotten too when they sleep is the rope
coiled neat as a molecule within
night's body, every rung
imprinted in us now.
Overhead a tree whirls
across the sky. A tree of stars
where our children stir and dream

they are flying from limb to limb
among the shining creatures taking shape
the moment the mind makes them out—
The Hunter, two Bears, the Princess, the Swan,
dance on the dark floor of heaven.
Dance like the light that leaps in our eyes
when our children climb down from the tree at dawn.

—George Keithley

THREE

Nesting Dolls

Jennifer wants
to put the baby in
the big one
first and doesn't know
what to do with
the others after
that. They fit
inside each other but
she ends up with two:
one with the baby, one
with all the rest.

Do you have any candy?
I offer her fruit
and cheese. *Laura
brings me candy,
Saturday,* says Jennifer.
Her mother is Laura.

She calls me Mama
and she calls
her grandma Mama
and the girls
her father dates
are Mama, to Jennifer,
who is trying
to put a family of
nesting dolls in their places
and she doesn't know
where the baby one
belongs.

—Neva Hacker

JANE'S GIFTS

Jane gave the best gifts.
Every Christmas we would eagerly open the box.
Just the wrapping and the ties
took your breath away.
Inside on Christmas morning
would be leather wallets
when all you'd had was plastic
or a blouse you knew you'd wear for best.
She always remembered your favorite colors.
Or what set off your eyes.
Sometimes in a given year
Jane's gifts would be all I'd have
that didn't come from Sears.
She told me one Christmas
after the children had opened their just right gifts
that she and Ray had visited me
when I was three
boarded in a foster home.
They had seen my very neat little cot
with a very neat little bear
with a very neat little dresser.
They had wanted to take me in their arms.
But they hadn't.
They had talked about adopting me.
But they didn't.
For years my mother bad-mouthed
her so-called rich and uncaring doctor brother.
Quietly and thankfully I opened
Jane's richly and carefully tied gifts.
When my mother was alive, my mother was my mother.
I was not up for adoption.
Quietly, without words, now that she is gone
Jane and I have adopted each other.

—Nora Ruth Roberts

CONJUGATION

The Latin teacher wore flowers
with plaids. We knew she'd never marry.

Black and white were concerts
and church, colors that mixed only

on formal occasions. Mother's
answer to What if your daughter—?

was Looks, as in you never
wore purple and red together.

Everything in its place: now and then,
salt and pepper, treble and bass—

In the movies, and in those weddings
where everything matches, we feel better

about ourselves, we feel like Us.
Violets on that blouse, in little bunches.

—Martha Collins

What Difference Does It Make?

When the giant panda views another
of her species through a window, in a mirror,
does she feel a little less lonely?
I smile when I see another couple like us,
though of course they aren't like us,
except for the contrast
between white skin, and black.

The year I turned twelve
the way we live was still a crime.
Then Loving vs. Virginia made race irrelevant
in marriage, told Richard and Mildred they could live
where they were born.

I thought it nothing to write about,
only one kind of difference in a world of difference,
no shame and nothing to brandish like a badge.
I thought that what should not matter, did not.

An *odd couple*,
all she could get, a trophy, a burden.
Has he bought my whiteness with his maleness?
Or does his blackness accompany my womanhood
in the same swampy place?

Through his eyes I see the pain
of interviews that go well on the phone,
the patronage of compliments followed by *for a...*
But I can choose not to see it at all,
as my white skin carries me like a sail.

If you flayed us, you'd notice only the sex,
but it's impossible to live without skin.

Whenever I blurt the word "racist,"
I want to retrieve it, as when
I called a child, "illegitimate";
that night my husband asked,

"What difference does it make?"

Epithets are helicopters
with swords for blades,
but also methods of transport
from here to there.

What our families didn't say and do
was not kind, and then we grew through it like a tree
whose roots invade sewer lines.
Good things—eating, learning, love—
demand openings, penetration,
marriage.
To let the other in,
to not say, *not us*.

—Natasha Sajé

BABYSITTING AT THE PLAINSMAN MOTEL

I knock, think how this child's home
should be rented by the night, $14.95
at the drive-thru window
for truckers with only a few hours to go,
lovers moaning through the bathroom wall.

She answers the door herself
and sits me down on the checkered bedspread,
punches cards from her magazine.
Put our pennies here, she tells me, pointing
to the game-board centerfold's START.
I do it, watch her scan the winding cardboard path
scattered with hearts, math books, and syringes,
bottles of rust-colored liquor, a plastic infant.

We try to get to here
before time runs out, she tells me,
pointing at the last red square
with a mortarboard slanted across.
OK, I tell her, and search the walls
for bookshelves, listen to the roar
of traffic through her window.

She rolls the dice as she tells me
how her brothers count seconds between cars
in the front yard, dash in between, their bodies
blue-jeanned blades of adrenalin
zig-zagging from Don's Burgers
to the median, and back.

She moves and takes her first card, asks
Do you worry about your family
dying? I nod, ask her to repeat
the directions, to read her card aloud,
to roll the dice again.

—Alissa Reardon

EXILE'S CHILD

I asked my father
permission to kill a fly.
Then I came back and asked
—could I kill another?
He thought for a while
and said—No. Evening was taking
the sting off a family outing.
Along the beach, cousins
were charring meat. The waves
were turning an intense No-color.
I asked him if he'd killed anyone
in the old country: he said—No.
Then I was enraged at him,
feeling he was asleep, like the sand,
like the striped umbrella whose shadow
fell at right angles to night,
like my serious brother toting sums
in a leatherbound ledger: only the flies
were awake, and their drone,
fainter than surf, was audible
only when I sat and held my breath
stock-still by the banked coals.

—D. Nurkse

Four Hours

My sister picks up her daughters at the bus stop
ever since a nine-year-old girl from the neighborhood
was coaxed into a car by a man
telling her he'd hit a kitten down the road.
His story went that the small ball of fur
ran somewhere near the railroad tracks
and he needed an extra pair of eyes to find it.
The girl was smart and had been taught
everything grownups thought she'd have to know
about even the worst of strangers, but she wanted
to be a veterinarian when she grew up.
And the man looked as though he'd been crying.
"He had that child in the car four hours,"
my mother tells me, my mother who would cut off his balls
if she had the chance. She sounds ugly, fed up, middle-class,
when she says it, and I want to say "No,"
but I too share her sentiment. My father
thinks the rapist deserves worse, to be shot dead—
no questions asked. My brother-in-law has a gun,
and my sister knows he'd use it if anyone tried to touch
their daughters, my nieces, my parents' grandchildren.
Four hours is longer than some double features,
longer than some continental plane rides,
longer than a whole afternoon in grade school.
Nothing is slower than time when you're nine years old,
nothing is more fragile than trust.
The rapist dropped the girl off at the pizza parlor
where the men who worked there called an ambulance.
Before this, my nieces walked the short distance home
and they protest, wanting to know why they can't anymore.
The after-school rapist hasn't been caught,
but the second and fifth grade rumors aren't terrifying enough.
My sister wonders how to tell her daughters,
who love small animals and only want to help.

—Denise Duhamel

WHERE GOD LIVES

It is hard to believe in God, even now.
He was always somewhere else.
Maybe fishing. And sometimes I get mad.
Like when my sister was eight
and I was six. Daddy went drinking,
left us all alone with my baby brothers.
We were potty-training the chubby one, Ben.

I went to pull him off his potty seat
and his weenie got caught in a crack
of blue plastic. Blood spurted as if I'd
chopped a hen's neck. My sister ran.
All four of us crying now and me holding
Ben's poor wiener
like a bloody worm in a washcloth.

I begged God to stop warm ooze soaking
through to my palm, and held Ben,
who yelped louder than Sam the day
we shut his tail in the closet. *I'm sorry,*
please God, help us. I chanted my prayer.
The way you do when you see the train's face
frothing in the tracks, yellow eyes and teeth
hissing the dark, and your car's stalled,
all the doors locked tight.

Our screen door whined, slammed
when my sister brought the women
in their gingham blouses. They found Vaseline
in our cupboards, rocked Ben until he slept,
gave us an orange popsicle, threw
the potty seat in the trash.

It is difficult to believe in God, even now.
But I want to say that day, when I was six

and holding what was left of my brother's dick
in my right hand, God's hair was in pin curls
under a red bandana. He had two names:
Elsie and Janet May. He lived on our street:
the four hundred block in the projects.
He was home; it was August and too hot for trout.

—Jeanne Bryner

FAMILY GATHERING

For Reva McDaniel Huey

In the woods behind our house,
there's a rock the size of a schoolbus,
grey-blue and covered with lichens.
My family stands in the shadow
of this rock, awkward as strangers.
My father holds the plastic container
away from his body, my aunt Norah
sobs so she is barely able to stand,
and to break this freezing silence
my mother clears her throat
and tells how she asked my favorite memory
and I said Grandma's blueberry pie.
My uncle Stanley shifts from foot to foot,
my aunt Naoma smiles a thin arrow,
my mother squeezes my hand,
and we begin.

              My father peels the lid
from the plastic container, reaches in,
and tosses gracefully. Ashes fall
in a gentle arc, land with a pattering like rain.
My father moves among us
holding the container like an offering plate.
Stanley throws a handful that stays together
until it lands at the foot of a sweetgum tree
and scatters. Naoma tosses underhand,
like throwing a softball. Norah shakes
her head, still sobbing. *I can't
believe this*, she says. Her hand darts forward,
quick as a garter snake,
and she pushes a handful into the air.
My mother lingers, letting the ashes
sift through her fingers like flour.
It is my turn. My father waits before me.
I want to reach into the container,

grab a fistful and throw it far from me,
so far I never see it land. I want to,
but I can't. My father moves on.
Next, my brother Silas, who's never been afraid
of anything. I envy him as his fingers dip
into the gritty ash and come out clean.
We are finished,

               but the container
isn't empty. We watch silently,
and my father pours the rest of the ashes
in a wide circle around us.
Breeze slips between us, whispering,
and as we turn and gather courage to leave,
my mouth fills with the taste of blueberry pie,
juicy, steaming, and so sweet.

—Amorak Huey

WALKING IN HOLCOMB GARDENS

To my mother

Let's say we choose what we take in
not from want or even need
but from something left undone
(paint cans on the floor   paper never hung
a million dreams woken up too soon).

Two rose-pinked mushrooms.
This great red oak.
A silver butterfly preening on my thumb.

Six hands around couldn't latch this puzzle closed.

Mushrooms. Butterfly. Oak.
Rune stones flung together.
The spell of a witch's brew

and once more
steam fills the kitchen on Wadsworth Avenue
from handkerchiefs boiling on the stove
from clouds in a pot of starch, and you,
plying the yellow soap on Monday's board,
rub again at all our weekly sins
twisting your heavy arms, wringing
through the lined palms of your hands
what last wet remains in a cotton blouse.

I sit at the table swinging my legs
eating the egg sandwich you fixed
between the last rinse and the bluing
adoring you like Cinderella's child

and then as suddenly
as from a castle's secret wall
you step out from behind the forbidden closet door
you dressed behind in your good black dress,

its square neck spread low and faced in satin.
The pillow flesh dipping in and out of its
own dizzy crease, trembling in the spotlight
of a pair of rhinestone clips, so beautiful—
so rare, this bow to the flesh

we cheeped around you like your birds.

Today, walking across this vast expanse
of lawn I hear the trains blow from
some distant place pulling freight
up impossible hills. Two thousand miles
away, you come tugging at my memory,
flashing for my attention wherever I look.

Mama, what's been left undone?
Where's the door we didn't close?
What silver child never grown
comes through now
fluttering at my fingers?

I lean against this red oak
whose rich vertical heart has pulled water
for over four hundred years and must know.

What dream needs finishing? what story told?
Whose child rocks her forehead
against this rough and silent tree
weeping for her mother?

—Alice Friman

CONTRIBUTORS

Judi K. Beach has published a chapbook, *Double Vision*, and her poems appear in *Tar River Poetry*, *Cape Rock*, *Earth's Daughters*, *Plainsong*, and the anthology, *Life on the Line: Selections on Words and Healing*.

Jeanne Bryner is an emergency room nurse and an English major in the Honors College of Kent State University. She has won many awards for her writing, and her poems appear in *Poetry East*, *Prairie Schooner*, *West Branch*, and *Black Warrior Review*.

Penny Cagan is a graduate of New York University's program in Creative Writing. Her poems have appeared in *Calyx*, *The New York Quarterly*, *Bone & Flesh*, *Words* (Scotland), and *The Lancashire Poetry Review*.

Martha Collins's third book of poems, *A History of Small Life on a Windy Planet*, won the Alice Fay Di Castagnola Award for work-in-progress and was published in 1993 by the University of Georgia Press. She directs the Creative Writing Program at U. Mass.-Boston.

Geraldine Connolly is the author of *The Red Room*, Heatherstone, and *Food for the Winter*, Purdue University Press. She has won fellowships from the National Endowment for the Arts, Yaddo, and the Maryland Arts Council.

Peter Cooley has published five books of poetry, the latest of which is *The Astonished Hours*, Carnegie Mellon University Press, 1992. He teaches creative writing at Tulane University. Recent poems appear in *The New Yorker*, *Poetry*, *Atlantic*, *Antaeus*, and *The Nation*.

Barbara Crooker has published five books of poems, the latest of which is *Obbligato*, Linwood Publishing, 1992. *Moving Poems* is forthcoming from Camel Press. Her poems appear in *Poet & Critic*, *The Christian Science Monitor*, *Passages North*, *West Branch*, and many anthologies.

Sean Thomas Dougherty's books include *Sunset by the Chain-Link Fence*, Red Dancefloor Press. He is co-founder and editor of *Red Brick Review* which received a 1993 Gregory Kolovakos Seedgrant from the Council of Literary Magazines and Presses.

Hilda Downer's book of poetry, *Bandana Creek*, published by Red Clay Press in 1979, recounts her life in the Appalachian mountains of North Carolina. She works as a part-time English instructor at Appalachian State University and as a psychiatric nurse.

Denise Duhamel is the author of *The Woman with Two Vaginas*, Salmon Run Publishers, 1994, *Smile!*, Warm Spring Press, 1992, and the forthcoming *Girl Soldier*, Garden Street Press, 1995. Her work appears in *Mondo Barbie* and *The Best American Poetry 1993* and *1994*.

Alice B. Fogel's *I Love This Dark World* will appear in 1995 from Zoland Books which published her first collection, *Elemental*. Her poems appear in *The Boston Review*, *Iowa Review*, and *Best American Poetry 1993*. She teaches writing at the University of New Hampshire.

Alice Friman's latest collection is *Driving for Jimmy Wonderland*, Barnwood Press, 1992. She has won the Consuelo Ford (1988), the Cecil Hemley (1990), and the Lucille Medwick Memorial Award (1993) from the Poetry Society of America, as well as the 1993 Abiko Quarterly Poetry Award.

John Gilgun's books include *From the Inside Out*, 1991, *The Dooley Poems*, 1991, *Music I Never Dreamed Of*, 1989, *Everything That Has Been Shall Be Again: The Reincarnation Fables of John Gilgun*, and a forthcoming book of stories, *Your Buddy Misses You*.

CONTRIBUTORS

Neva Hacker's poems appear in *Denver Quarterly, razzmatazz, South Coast Poetry Journal, Embers,* and *Bottomfish.* She has a story in *Mediphors* and also publishes articles. Until recently she was the director of a shelter for victims of domestic violence.

C.J. Hannah's novel, *Ashes to the Wind,* was published by Avon. Other work appears in *Thema, Poetry Motel, Rockford Review,* and *Arts Magazine.* A short story collection, *The Holy City Zoo,* is in preparation. "I visualize my narrator as Huck Finn's great-great-great-grandson...."

Amorak Huey has published poetry, fiction, essays, and book reviews, most recently in *International Quarterly, Poetry: An American Heritage, Southern Living,* and *Travel South.* He has taught creative writing to women at Jefferson Correctional Institution in Monticello, Florida.

George Keithley has written six books of poems and two plays, including *The Donner Party,* which was a Book-of-the-Month Club selection. His latest book of poems, *Earth's Eye,* has just appeared from Story Line Press.

Nancy Roxbury Knutson's chapbook, *Nothing Should Fall to Waste,* won the Arts Wayland Foundation Artist Wreath Award in 1983. Her poems appear in *The American Poetry Review, Calyx, The Iowa Review, Nimrod,* and *River Poems: An Anthology.*

Norbert Krapf's latest poetry collection is *Somewhere in Southern Indiana. Blue-Eyed Grass: Poems of Germany* is forthcoming. He translates folktales from his ancestral Franconia and the early poems of Rilke. He also teaches at Long Island University, C.W. Post Campus.

Maxine Kumin's ten books of poems include *Looking for Luck,* 1992, *Nurture,* 1989, and *The Long Approach,* 1985. She was awarded the Pulitzer Prize for Poetry in 1973 for her book, *Up Country.* She also served as the Consultant in Poetry to the Library of Congress in 1981-82.

Zev Levinson used to sell flowers in Northern California. He now lives in North Carolina where he is getting an M.F.A. degree. His poems appear in *Alaska Quarterly Review, International Poetry Review,* and a new anthology, *Cattle Bones & Coke Machines,* from Smiling Dog Press.

Maria Theresa Maggi has an M.F.A. degree from University of California, Irvine. Her poems appear in *Alaska Quarterly Review, Florida Review,* and *Black Warrior Review.* She is working on her first collection, *The Blank World,* and teaches writing at the University of Idaho.

Cris Mazza's fiction includes *Exposed,* 1994, and *How to Leave a Country,* 1992, from Coffee House Press, as well as *Revelation Countdown,* 1993, *Is It Sexual Harassment Yet?,* 1991, and *Animal Acts,* 1989, from Fiction Collective Two.

Kirk Nesset's poems appear in *The Paris Review, Tampa Review, Witness,* and *High Plains Literary Review.* He teaches at Whittier College, and his book, *The Stories of Raymond Carver,* will appear from Ohio University Press in 1994. He is working on a novel, *Mud People.*

D. Nurkse's poetry collections include *Voices Over Water,* Graywolf Press, 1993, *Staggered Lights,* Owl Creek Press, 1990, and *Shadow Wars,* Hanging Loose Press, 1988.

Lee Patton's novel, *The Last Californians,* is forthcoming. His poems appear in *Massachusetts Review, Threepenny Review,* and several anthologies. He is also a prizewinning playwright whose plays include *The House Guest,* "Right to Life," and *Ivan, the Terrible.*

Deidre Pope received an M.F.A. from Cornell University. Her poems appear in *Northwest Review, Seattle Review,* and the *Beloit Poetry Journal.* She is the production/readings coordinator at The Loft, a literary center for writers in Minneapolis.

CONTRIBUTORS

Alissa Reardon earned her B.S. and M.F.A. degrees from Colorado State University. Her work appears in *Sycamore Review*, *Soundings East*, *Hawaii Review*, and *Indiana Review*.

Kjersti A. Reed received an M.F.A. from San Diego State University. Her poems appear in *New England Review*, *The Minnesota Review*, and *Common Wages*. She is finishing her first collection, *Notes on a Broken Chandelier*.

Susan Richardson has published poetry, fiction, and essays, most recently in *Pavement Saw* and *Mediphors*. She was founding editor of *Calypso: Journal of Narrative Poetry and Poetic Fiction*. She works as a physician's assistant at a naval clinic in San Diego.

Len Roberts's most recent poetry collections are *Counting the Black Angels*, U. of Illinois Press, 1994, and *Dangerous Angels*, Copper Beech Press, 1993. Recent poems appear in *Hudson Review*, *Paris Review*, and *The American Poetry Review*.

Nora Ruth Roberts teaches at Medgar Evars College. Her doctoral dissertation on three radical women writers of the thirties will be published by Garland. Her travel memoir, *The Voyage of Nora's Ark*, was published by Funk & Wagnalls.

Natasha Sajé won the Agnes Lynch Starrett prize for *Red Under the Skin*, U. Pittsburgh Press, 1994. She is writing her dissertation on the coquette figure in the American novel and co-editing an anthology of South Slav-American writing.

Dennis Saleh's most recent book of poems, *This Is Not Surrealism*, won the first chapbook competition from Willamette River Books, 1993. Other books include *First Z Poems*, Bieler Press, and *100 Chameleons*, New Rivers Press. He has poems in *Poetry*, *Paris Review*, and *TriQuarterly*.

Vivian Shipley's most recent books of poems are *Devil's Lane*, Negative Capability Press, and *Poems Out of Harlan County*, Ithaca House. She directs the writing program at Southern Connecticut State University and is editor of *Connecticut Review*.

Floyd Skloot's poetry collection, *Music Appreciation*, University Press of Florida, and his second novel, *Summer Blue*, Story Line Press, both appeared in 1994. He has an essay in *The Best American Essays of 1993*, and his work appears in *The American Scholar* and *Gettysburg Review*.

Mark Solomon, a recent graduate of the Warren Wilson M.F.A. program, is seeking a publisher for his first collection, *The Pleasure of a Ride*. His poems appear in *Broadway Boogie*, *Bomb*, *TriQuarterly*, and *Abiko Quarterly*.

Anne McCrary Sullivan taught high school for many years and is now a doctoral candidate at the University of Florida. She holds an M.F.A. from Warren Wilson, and her poems appear in *The Texas Review*, *Ariel*, and *The Gettysburg Review*. She is an editor at *English Journal*.

Frank Van Zant teaches English and coaches three sports in Rockville Centre, New York. His work appears in *Yankee*, *Rant*, *Long Island Quarterly*, *Sports Collector's Digest*, and *Fan Baseball Magazine*. He performs poetry as a member of Wordsmith & Co.

Gary J. Whitehead is a Pearl Hogrefe Fellow in Creative Writing at Iowa State University for 1994-5. He has poems forthcoming in *Yankee*. A teacher of developmentally disabled adults, he edits and publishes the Providence/Boston poetry journal, *Defined Providence*.

Slapering Hol Press

What's Become of Eden: Poems of Family at Century's End (1994)

2nd Edition (1999)

Chapbook Series

Islands   Andrew Krivak (1999)

The Last Campaign   Rachel Loden (1998)

No Pine Tree in This Forest Is Perfect   Ellen Goldsmith (1997)

Bonanza   Lynn McGee (1996)

Muscle & Bone   Paul-Victor Winters (1995)

Weathering   Pearl Karrer (1993)

River Poems: An Anthology (1992)

Note for a Missing Friend   Dina Ben-Lev (1991)

Voices from the River: An Anthology (1990)

THE HUDSON VALLEY
WRITERS' CENTER

The Hudson Valley Writers' Center is a non-profit organization dedicated to literacy, literary arts, and the remarkable literary heritage of our region. The Center presents public readings by established and emerging writers, offers a variety of workshops in many genres, collaborates with local schools, organizes educational programs for people with special needs, and publishes new works of literature under the imprint of Slapering Hol (Old Dutch for Sleepy Hollow) Press. The press was established in 1990 to provide opportunities for poets who have not yet appeared in book form and to publish poetry anthologies. The Hudson Valley Writers' Center is housed in the railroad station at Philipse Manor in Sleepy Hollow, New York. This building, which the Center has recently restored, is listed on the National and State Registers of Historic Places.